KT-443-648

Made from scratch

SOUP

EVERYDAY EASY HOME COOKING

This edition published by Parragon Books Ltd in 2014
LOVE FOOD is an imprint of Parragon Books Ltd

Parragon Books Ltd
Chartist House
15–17 Trim Street
Bath BA1 1HA, UK
www.parragon.com/lovefood

Copyright © Parragon Books Ltd 2012 – 2014

LOVE FOOD and the accompanying heart device is a registered trademark of
Parragon Books Ltd in Australia, the UK, USA, India and the EU.

All rights reserved. No part of this publication may be reproduced, stored
in a retrieval system or transmitted, in any form or by any means, electronic,
mechanical, photocopying, recording or otherwise, without the prior permission
of the copyright holder.

ISBN 978-1-4723-2994-3

Printed in China

Cover photography by Ian Garlick
Design by Geoff Borin
New photography by Clive Streeter
New recipes, introduction and notes by Rachel Carter
Nutritional analysis by Fiona Hunter

Notes for the Reader
This book uses both metric and imperial measurements. Follow the same
units of measurement throughout; do not mix metric and imperial. All spoon
measurements are level: teaspoons are assumed to be 5 ml, and tablespoons
are assumed to be 15 ml. Unless otherwise stated, milk is assumed to be full fat,
eggs and individual vegetables are medium, and pepper is freshly ground black
pepper. Unless otherwise stated, all root vegetables should be peeled prior to
using.

Garnishes, decorations and serving suggestions are all optional and not
necessarily included in the recipe ingredients or method. Any optional
ingredients and seasoning to taste are not included in the nutritional analysis. The
times given are an approximate guide only. Preparation times differ according
to the techniques used by different people and the cooking times may also vary
from those given. Optional ingredients, variations or serving suggestions have not
been included in the time calculations.

Contents

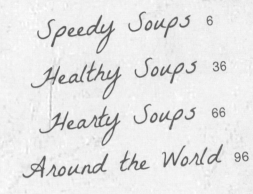

Introduction

Whether you need a comforting winter warmer, a light summer bite or a quick and easy weeknight dinner – soup is the ideal solution to mealtime dilemmas. Easy to make, great for leftovers and packed with nutritious ingredients, it's a filling and endlessly adaptable part of any cook's repertoire.

Few dishes are as versatile as soup – they are an economical way of using storecupboard staples and leftover foods, and often are a quick, fuss-free meal that can be made with ease. Soup can also be a simple way to include health-boosting ingredients in your diet – packed with vegetables, and often low in saturated fat, they are a good go-to meal whether you're watching your weight or not. Plus, with the addition of grains, pulses, pastas and noodles, soup is a great way to stay fuller for longer – keeping hunger pangs at bay with these added carbohydrates.

Soups can be served as a palate cleanser before a big meal, between courses, as a light starter before a rich main course or as a substantial meal in a bowl all by itself. They are great for lunch and serve as the ideal midday energy booster.

The chapters of this book include Speedy Soups which contains recipes that are ready to go in under an hour, and require a minimal amount of pre-cooking preparation. Healthy Soups are ideal for anyone keeping an eye on their food intake, as all the recipes are low in calories or saturated fat but still filled with ingredients to keep you satisfied until dinner. Hearty Soups includes substantial meal-in-a-bowl soups with pasta and pulses. There are also some classic puréed soups containing root vegetables and squashes, which are at their best in the colder months. The Around the World chapter has a selection of some of the best international soup recipes.

With minimal ingredients, prep and a simple on-the-hob cooking process, soups are a good fuss-free meal full of nutrients to slot into busy lifestyles.

Storecupboard Essentials

• Basic Vegetables

Onions (try buying them diced and frozen, to save yourself time), garlic and ginger (which are also available in long-life jars or frozen), celery, leeks and carrots are all ideal for making a flavourful base for soup.

• Ready-made Stock

There is a huge variety of stock options readily available from the supermarket – there are frozen 'shots', fresh tubs of liquid stock, dried stock cubes, tins of dried stock powder and concentrated

stock pots. Keep a selection if you can, but chicken and vegetable stock cubes are a definite storecupboard essential.

• Oils

There is no need to use expensive extra virgin olive oil in soup. A basic rapeseed, olive or vegetable oil, that is neutral in flavour, is preferable.

• Flavourings

Keep good quality sea salt and whole black peppercorns, as these give a good depth of flavour. Other basic condiments that often come in useful include balsamic vinegar, tomato purée, dark soy sauce, miso paste, mustard (French and wholegrain), ketchup and Worcestershire sauce, which also make great savoury additions. There are also new 'umami' pastes available – Parmesan and dried porcini mushrooms in this give a hit of savoury flavour that complements both vegetable- and meat-based soups.

• Pulses

Whether you choose dried or canned pulses, these should always be on hand as they add bulk and flavour and are both nutritious and easy on the budget. Remember that not all dried pulses need to be soaked before using – split peas, red lentils and adzuki beans can be added directly to the soup after a quick rinse in cold water. Keep a small selection of

canned beans, such as borlotti, cannellini, chickpeas and butter beans, as a standby for bulking out hearty soups in the winter months.

• Dried Herbs & Spices

A well-stocked larder of dried spices should include smoked paprika, curry powder, cumin seeds, ground coriander, cumin, dried chillies or chilli flakes and black peppercorns. Woody herbs such as rosemary, thyme and oregano retain their flavour well in a dried format but leafy herbs like coriander, basil and parsley are best used fresh.

• Canned & Bottled Ingredients

Canned tomatoes are an essential item on the weekly shop, and these are now available with extra flavourings, such as basil and garlic, which can save time. Sun-dried tomatoes in olive oil or ready-roasted peppers in brine, olives, capers, pesto and anchovies are also very useful to keep at home.

• Dried Pasta & Noodles

Dried soup pasta and most noodles are an ideal addition to soups (especially broths). You can also use regular dried pasta, but this takes longer to cook. Both pasta and noodles are handy as they have a long shelf life and a neutral flavour which sits well with stronger soups.

Tomato Soup *8*

Leek & Potato Soup *10*

Pea Soup *12*

Fishermen's Soup *14*

Chilled Avocado Soup *16*

Ham & Lentil Soup *18*

Lemon, Chicken & Rice Soup *20*

Carrot & Parsnip Soup *22*

Tuscan Bean Soup *24*

Cabbage & Smoky Bacon Soup *26*

Spicy Sweetcorn Chowder *28*

Chicken, Avocado & Chipotle Soup *30*

Mixed Squash Soup *32*

Spicy Chicken Noodle Soup *34*

Speedy Soups

Tomato Soup

 SERVES 4

PREP TIME:
5 minutes

COOKING TIME:
10–15 minutes

nutritional information
per serving   100 kcals, 6g fat, 0.8g sat fat, 5.5g total sugars, 0.4g salt

This soup is ready in minutes and made with storecupboard ingredients, perfect for a warming lunch or a quick starter.

INGREDIENTS

2 tbsp olive oil
1 large onion, chopped
400 g/14 oz canned whole plum tomatoes
300 ml/10 fl oz vegetable stock
1 tbsp tomato purée
1 tsp hot pepper sauce
handful of fresh basil leaves
salt and pepper

1. Heat the oil in a large saucepan over a medium heat, then add the onion and fry for 4–5 minutes, stirring, until soft. Add the tomatoes, stock, tomato purée, hot pepper sauce and half the basil leaves.

2. Process using a hand-held blender until smooth. Stir the soup over a medium heat until just boiling, then season to taste with salt and pepper.

3. Serve the soup in warmed serving bowls, garnished with the remaining basil leaves.

GOES WELL WITH *Toasted wholemeal bread and grated mature Cheddar cheese.*

Leek & Potato Soup

 SERVES 6

PREP TIME:
15 minutes

COOKING TIME:
20–25 minutes

nutritional information per serving	195 kcals, 13g fat, 8g sat fat, 3g total sugars, 0.6g salt

This is a classic British soup and its velvety texture and mild flavours are great for warming you up in the depths of winter - especially as this is when leeks are at their best flavour and price.

INGREDIENTS

55 g/2 oz butter

1 onion, chopped

3 leeks, sliced

225 g/8 oz potatoes, cut into 2-cm/¾-inch cubes

850 ml/1½ pints vegetable stock

salt and pepper

150 ml/5 fl oz single cream, to serve

snipped fresh chives, to garnish

1. Melt the butter in a large saucepan over a medium heat, add the onion, leeks and potatoes and sauté gently for 2–3 minutes, until soft but not brown. Pour in the stock, bring to the boil, then reduce the heat and simmer, covered, for 15 minutes.

2. Process using a hand-held blender, until smooth.

3. Heat the soup gently and season to taste with salt and pepper. Ladle into warmed bowls, garnish with a swirl of cream and snipped chives and serve immediately.

This soup is great
to have as a freezer
standby. Simply chill
after cooking, pour into
an airtight container or
a large jug lined with
a plastic food bag.
Seal and freeze for
up to 3 months.

Pea Soup

SERVES 4

PREP TIME:
15 minutes

COOKING TIME:
20–30 minutes

nutritional information
per serving   274 kcals, 16g fat, 10g sat fat, 3.5g total sugars, 0.9g salt

Peas are the essence of summer and their sweet flavour works so well in soup. Topped with crumbled Roquefort and crispy croûtons, this is a mouth-watering delight.

INGREDIENTS

40 g/1½ oz butter
4 tbsp finely chopped shallots
1 litre/1¾ pints vegetable stock or water
400 g/14 oz shelled peas
pinch of sugar
4 tbsp crème fraîche
salt and pepper
croûtons and blue cheese, such as Roquefort, crumbled, to serve

1. Melt the butter in a large saucepan over a medium heat. Add the shallots and fry for 2–3 minutes, or until soft. Add the stock, peas, sugar, and salt and pepper to taste and bring to the boil, uncovered. Simmer for 15–20 minutes, or until the peas are tender.

2. Strain the peas and reserve the cooking liquid. Process the peas in a food processor or blender, until smooth, then return the purée to the pan. Gradually stir in the cooking liquid until you have the desired consistency.

3. Reheat the soup; do not boil. Stir in the crème fraîche and adjust the seasoning, if necessary. Serve immediately with blue cheese and croûtons sprinkled over.

1   2   2

COOK'S NOTE

Use either frozen or freshly shelled peas in this recipe. If preferred, swap the Roquefort for a milder blue cheese, like Stilton.

Fishermen's Soup

SERVES 6

PREP TIME:
10 minutes

COOKING TIME:
20–25 minutes

nutritional information per serving	333 kcals, 20g fat, 3g sat fat, 4g total sugars, 0.3g salt

Use your own choice of firm white fish - teamed with crusty bread this soup makes a complete meal in a flash.

INGREDIENTS

900 g/2 lb fillets of mixed white fish, such as cod, flounder, halibut, monkfish, sea bass and whiting, and peeled prawns

150 ml/5 fl oz olive oil

2 large onions, sliced

2 stalks celery, thinly sliced

2 cloves garlic, chopped

150 ml/5 fl oz white wine

4 tomatoes, chopped

pared rind of 1 orange

1 tsp chopped fresh thyme

2 tbsp chopped fresh parsley

2 bay leaves

salt and pepper

croûtons and lemon wedges, to serve

1. Cut the fish into fairly large chunks, discarding any skin. Heat the oil in a saucepan, add the onion, celery and garlic and fry for 5 minutes, or until softened.

2. Add the fish and prawns to the pan, then add the wine, tomatoes, orange rind, herbs and bay leaves. Season to taste with salt and pepper and add enough cold water to cover. Bring to the boil, then simmer, uncovered, for 15 minutes, or until the fish is cooked through and flakes easily.

3. Remove and discard the bay leaves. Ladle into warmed bowls and serve immediately, with croûtons and lemon wedges.

1

1
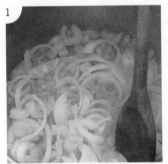

2

COOK'S NOTE

Use frozen pre-prepared fish in this recipe for convenience and speed. Just ensure that it has thawed completely before adding to the pan.

Chilled Avocado Soup

 SERVES 4

PREP TIME:
10 minutes
plus chilling

COOKING TIME:
No cooking

nutritional information
per serving

311 kcals, 29g fat, 12g sat fat, 2g total sugars, 0.4g salt

On a hot day, this soup is the perfect refreshing starter to a relaxing summer meal. Serve thoroughly chilled.

INGREDIENTS

2 avocados

1 tbsp lemon juice

1 tbsp snipped fresh chives,
plus extra to garnish

1 tbsp chopped fresh
flat-leaf parsley

425 ml/15 fl oz chicken stock,
chilled

300 ml/10 fl oz single cream,
plus extra to serve

dash of Worcestershire sauce

salt and pepper

1. Halve the avocados and remove the stones. Scoop out the flesh and chop roughly.

2. Place the avocado flesh, lemon juice, chives, parsley, stock, cream and Worcestershire sauce in the blender and process until smooth. Season to taste with salt and pepper.

3. Transfer the soup to a bowl, cover, and chill until required. Serve with single cream drizzled over the soup, topped with snipped chives.

1   2   3

COOK'S NOTE
The soup is best
consumed within
a couple of hours
of making and is
delicious served
with seafood
such as crab or
prawns.

Ham & Lentil Soup

SERVES 2

PREP TIME:
10 minutes

COOKING TIME:
25–30 minutes

nutritional information per serving	374 kcals, 11.5g fat, 2.5g sat fat, 5.5g total sugars, 3.5g salt

Transform cold cooked ham into a healthy, hearty winter meal packed with goodness that will leave you feeling full and contented.

INGREDIENTS

200 g/7 oz cooked ham

1 tbsp vegetable oil

1 onion, finely chopped

1 clove garlic, finely chopped

1 carrot, finely diced

1 stick celery, thinly sliced

400 g/14 oz canned cooked green lentils, drained

1 tsp finely chopped fresh rosemary leaves,

600 ml/1 pint vegetable or ham stock

pepper

1. Using two forks, finely shred the cooked ham and set aside.

2. Heat the oil in a saucepan over a medium–high heat. Add the onion, garlic, carrot and celery and sauté for 4–5 minutes, or until starting to soften.

3. Add the cooked lentils, rosemary, shredded ham and stock, and season to taste with pepper. Cover and simmer for 20 minutes, or until the vegetables are just tender. Serve immediately.

1 2 3

FREEZING TIP
Freeze for up
to 6 months in an
airtight container.
Defrost completely
and re-heat to serve.

Lemon, Chicken & Rice Soup

 SERVES 4

PREP TIME:
10 minutes

COOKING TIME:
15–20 minutes

nutritional information per serving	341 kcals, 6.5g fat, 1.5g sat fat, 3g total sugars, 0.9g salt

This soup is packed with fresh flavours - lifted by a zingy dose of lemon juice.

INGREDIENTS

1 tbsp vegetable oil

1 onion, finely chopped

1 leek, finely chopped

1 clove garlic, crushed

finely grated zest and juice of ½ lemon

100 g/3½ oz basmati rice

1 litre/1¾ pints chicken stock

2 cooked chicken breasts, roughly chopped

100 g/3½ oz fresh spinach

175 g/6 oz frozen peas

4 tbsp chopped fresh flat-leaf parsley

salt and pepper

Parmesan cheese, to serve

1. Heat the oil in a large saucepan over a medium heat. Sauté the onion and leek for 4–5 minutes, until starting to soften. Add the garlic and lemon zest and cook for a further 1–2 minutes.

2. Add the rice and stock and bring to the boil. Cover and simmer for 8 minutes. Add the chicken, spinach and peas and season to taste with salt and pepper. Cook for a further 4 minutes until the rice is cooked through.

3. Stir in the lemon juice and parsley and serve with some Parmesan cheese shavings scattered on top.

1

2

3

COOK'S NOTE
Only add the
lemon juice when
you are just
about to serve the
soup, as it will
cause the green
vegetables to
lose their colour.

Carrot & Parsnip Soup

SERVES 6

PREP TIME:
10 minutes

COOKING TIME:
30–35 minutes

nutritional information per serving	92 kcals, 1g fat, 0.2g sat fat, 8g total sugars, 0.4g salt

Carrots and parsnips are both naturally sweet and they make great soup. The chervil's flavour adds a delicious freshness to this light and simple recipe.

INGREDIENTS

350 g/12 oz carrots, chopped
350 g/12 oz parsnips, chopped
4 shallots, chopped
4 fresh chervil sprigs
850 ml/1½ pints vegetable stock
salt and pepper
double cream, to garnish

1. Put the carrots, parsnips, shallots and chervil into a saucepan, pour in the stock and season with salt and pepper. Bring to the boil, reduce the heat and simmer for 20–25 minutes, until the vegetables are tender.

2. Remove the pan from the heat and leave to cool slightly. Remove and discard the chervil, then transfer to a food processor or blender, in batches if necessary, and process until smooth.

3. Return the soup to the rinsed-out pan and reheat gently; do not boil. Ladle into warmed bowls, swirl about 1 tablespoon of cream on the top of each and serve.

1 2 3

COOK'S NOTE
If you prefer,
don't peel the carrots
and parsnips - a
quick scrub will
suffice.

Tuscan Bean Soup

SERVES 6

PREP TIME:
5 minutes

COOKING TIME:
25–30 minutes

nutritional information
per serving

270 kcals, 8g fat, 1.5g sat fat, 0.5g total sugars, 0.3g salt

A fantastic storecupboard recipe, ready in minutes and with virtually no preparation necessary.

INGREDIENTS

300 g/10½ oz canned cannellini beans, drained and rinsed

300 g/10½ oz canned borlotti beans, drained and rinsed

about 600 ml/1 pint chicken or vegetable stock

115 g/4 oz dried soup pasta

4 tbsp olive oil

2 cloves garlic, very finely chopped

3 tbsp chopped fresh flat-leaf parsley

salt and pepper

1. Place half the cannellini and half the borlotti beans in a food processor or blender with half the stock and process until smooth. Pour into a large saucepan and add the remaining beans. Stir in enough of the remaining stock to achieve the desired consistency, then bring to the boil.

2. Add the pasta and return to the boil, then reduce the heat and cook for 15 minutes, or until just tender.

3. Meanwhile, heat 3 tablespoons of the oil in a small frying pan. Add the garlic and cook, stirring constantly, for 2–3 minutes, or until golden. Stir the garlic into the soup with the parsley.

4. Season to taste with salt and pepper and ladle into warmed bowls. Drizzle with the remaining oil and serve immediately.

1   2   3

Cabbage & Smoky Bacon Soup

 SERVES 4   PREP TIME: 15 minutes   COOKING TIME: 25–30 minutes

nutritional information per serving   330 kcals, 18.5g fat, 6g sat fat, 8.5g total sugars, 2.9g salt

A full-flavoured soup that packs a punch – perfect served with warm tear-and-share bread or some crispy croûtes.

INGREDIENTS

1 tbsp vegetable oil
2 cloves garlic, crushed
1 onion, finely chopped
2 sticks celery, chopped
250 g/9 oz smoked bacon lardons
1 Savoy cabbage, cored and shredded
1.3 litres/2¼ pints chicken stock
1 tsp Worcestershire sauce
pepper
2 tbsp chopped fresh flat-leaf parsley, to serve

1. Heat the oil in a large frying pan over a medium–high heat. Add the garlic, onion and celery and sauté for 4–5 minutes, or until softened.

2. Add the bacon and fry for a further 3–4 minutes, or until starting to brown.

3. Add the cabbage, stock and Worcestershire sauce and season to taste with pepper. Cover and simmer for 15–20 minutes.

4. Process in a blender or food processor, until smooth. Serve with the parsley scattered over.

2

3

4

Spicy Sweetcorn Chowder

 SERVES 6   PREP TIME: 15 minutes   COOKING TIME: 30–35 minutes

nutritional information per serving	188 kcals, 5.5g fat, 0.8g sat fat, 6.5g total sugars, 0.5g salt

An unusual twist on a classic chowder. In this recipe silken tofu is puréed to give a creamy texture, which complements the vegetables and fresh herbs.

INGREDIENTS

1 tbsp olive oil
1 onion, diced
2 cloves garlic, finely chopped
2 carrots, diced
2 sticks celery, diced
1 red pepper, deseeded and diced
450 g/1 lb frozen sweetcorn
½ tsp chilli powder
1 litre/1¾ pints vegetable stock
225 g/8 oz silken tofu, drained
2 tbsp chopped coriander, to garnish
3 spring onions, thinly sliced, to garnish

1. Heat the oil in a large frying pan over a medium–high heat. Add the onion and garlic and cook, stirring occasionally, for about 5 minutes or until soft.

2. Add the carrots, celery, pepper, sweetcorn, chilli powder and stock. Bring to the boil, reduce the heat to medium–low and simmer, uncovered, for about 20 minutes or until the vegetables are soft.

3. Process the tofu together with a ladleful of the soup in a blender or food processor, until smooth. Stir the tofu mixture into the soup and simmer for 5 minutes, or until heated through. Serve hot, garnished with the coriander and spring onions.

Chicken, Avocado & Chipotle Soup

SERVES 6   PREP TIME: 10 minutes   COOKING TIME: 5 minutes

nutritional information per serving	166 kcals, 5.5g fat, 1.5g sat fat, 0.3g total sugars, 0.8g salt

This light but spicy chicken broth is a perfect lunchtime bite for hot summer days.

INGREDIENTS

1.5 litres/2¾ pints chicken stock

2–3 cloves garlic, finely chopped

1–2 dried chipotle chillies, thinly sliced

1 avocado

juice of ½ lime

3–5 spring onions, thinly sliced

350–400 g/12–14 oz cooked chicken breast, torn into bite-sized pieces

2 tbsp chopped fresh coriander

1 lime, cut into wedges, to serve

1. Place the stock in a large saucepan with the garlic and chillies and bring to the boil.

2. Meanwhile, cut the avocado in half around the stone. Twist apart, then remove the stone with a knife. Remove and discard the skin, dice the flesh and toss in the lime juice to prevent discoloration.

3. Arrange the spring onions, chicken, avocado and coriander in warmed bowls.

4. Ladle hot stock over and serve immediately with lime wedges.

1   2   2

GOES WELL WITH
Serve with lightly
salted tortilla
chips - they
are the perfect
antidote to the
heat of the chilli.

Mixed Squash Soup

 SERVES 4

PREP TIME:
10 minutes

COOKING TIME:
25–30 minutes

nutritional information
per serving · 169 kcals, 7g fat, 2.5g sat fat, 14.5g total sugars, 0.7g salt

Squashes make superb velvety-textured soups with vivid colours. Mixing the different types gives more interest and flavour so try buying a selection of what is in season.

INGREDIENTS

1 tbsp vegetable oil
1 large onion, chopped
1 stick celery, chopped
2 carrots, chopped
2 cloves garlic, crushed
800 g/1 lb 12 oz mixed squash, peeled, deseeded and cubed
1 litre/1¾ pints vegetable stock
1 tbsp fresh thyme leaves, finely chopped
salt and pepper
crème fraîche, to serve

1. Heat the oil in a large saucepan over a medium–high heat. Add the onion, celery and carrots and sweat for 3–4 minutes, or until starting to soften.

2. Add the garlic and squash, and sauté for a further minute. Add the stock and thyme and season to taste with salt and pepper. Bring to the boil, cover and simmer for 20 minutes, or until the vegetables are tender.

3. Process using a hand-held blender, until smooth. Serve immediately, topped with a dollop of crème fraîche.

1   2   3

GOES WELL WITH
Serve in the hollowed out crust of a cottage loaf. Remove the soft inside of the bread with a spoon and set aside to make croûtons to serve with the soup.

Spicy Chicken Noodle Soup

 SERVES 2

 PREP TIME:
15 minutes

COOKING TIME:
5–10 minutes

nutritional information
per serving

513 kcals, 10.5g fat, 2.5g sat fat, 8.5g total sugars, 2.1g salt

This quick, healthy, wholesome soup is a real winner for an instant meal that's packed with goodness. The main flavour comes from miso, a highly nutritious fermented paste used as the basis of many noodle soups.

INGREDIENTS

300 ml/10 fl oz chicken stock

1 x 18 g/¾ oz sachet miso paste

2-cm/¾-inch piece fresh ginger, peeled and finely grated

1 red chilli, deseeded and thinly sliced

1 carrot, cut into thin strips

200 g/7 oz pak choi, roughly chopped

150 g/5½ oz dried egg thread noodles, cooked

1 cooked chicken breast, shredded

dark soy sauce, to taste

4 spring onions, trimmed and finely chopped

1. Place the stock together with 250 ml/9 fl oz boiling water in a saucepan and bring to the boil over a medium–high heat. Add the miso paste and simmer for 1–2 minutes.

2. Add the ginger, chilli, carrot, pak choi, cooked noodles and chicken. Simmer for a further 4–5 minutes. Season to taste with soy sauce.

3. Scatter the spring onions in the base of two serving dishes and pour the soup over. Serve immediately.

Chunky Vegetable Soup *38*

Broccoli Soup *40*

Chicken Noodle Soup *42*

Roast Mediterranean Vegetable Soup *44*

Carrot, Celery & Apple Soup *46*

Beef & Barley Broth *48*

Roast Tomato & Pesto Soup *50*

Curried Courgette Soup *52*

Carrot & Coriander Soup *54*

Chipotle, Chicken & Bean Soup *56*

Spiced Pumpkin Soup *58*

Asparagus Soup *60*

Fennel & Summer Vegetable Soup *62*

Spicy Pepper & Tomato Soup *64*

Healthy Soups

Chunky Vegetable Soup

 SERVES 4   PREP TIME: 10 minutes   COOKING TIME: 15–20 minutes

nutritional information per serving   113 kcals, 6g fat, 0.7g sat fat, 8g total sugars, 0.4g salt

This is a hearty, satisfying soup that makes a colourful and nutritious lunch, any day of the week. Add seasonal veg to make a meal fit for any weather.

INGREDIENTS

1 red onion
1 stick celery
1 courgette
2 carrots
2 tbsp sunflower oil
400 g/14 oz canned chopped plum tomatoes
300 ml/10 fl oz vegetable stock
1 large sprig of fresh thyme
salt and pepper
chopped fresh thyme, to garnish

1. Cut the onion, celery, courgette and carrots into 1-cm/½-inch cubes.

2. Heat the oil in a large saucepan over a medium heat. Add the vegetables and sauté, stirring, for 5 minutes without browning.

3. Add the tomatoes, stock and the thyme sprig. Bring to the boil, then reduce the heat. Cover and simmer for 10–15 minutes, until the vegetables are just tender. Remove and discard the thyme sprig and season to taste with salt and pepper.

4. Transfer the soup to warmed serving bowls. Garnish with chopped thyme and serve immediately.

COOK'S NOTE
If fresh thyme is not available, use 1 teaspoon of dried thyme instead. A scattering of freshly chopped parsley is good for a fresh garnish.

Broccoli Soup

 SERVES 6   PREP TIME: 10 minutes   COOKING TIME: 25–30 minutes

nutritional information per serving	104 kcals, 0.7g fat, 0.1g sat fat, 1.5g total sugars, 0.5g salt

With few ingredients this soup is quick to whip up and ideal for using up leftover vegetables in the fridge.

INGREDIENTS

350 g/12 oz broccoli
1 leek, sliced
1 stick celery, sliced
1 clove garlic, crushed
350 g/12 oz potato, diced
1 litre/1¾ pints vegetable stock
1 bay leaf
pepper
toasted croûtons, to serve

1. Cut the broccoli into florets and set aside. Cut the thicker broccoli stalks into 1-cm/½-inch dice and put into a large saucepan with the leek, celery, garlic, potato, stock and bay leaf. Bring to the boil, then reduce the heat, cover and simmer for 15 minutes.

2. Add the broccoli florets to the soup and return to the boil. Reduce the heat, cover and simmer for a further 3–5 minutes, or until the potato and broccoli stalks are tender.

3. Remove from the heat and leave the soup to cool slightly. Remove and discard the bay leaf. Transfer to a food processor or blender, in batches if necessary, and process until smooth.

4. Return the soup to the saucepan and heat through thoroughly. Season to taste with pepper. Ladle the soup into warmed bowls and serve immediately with crusty bread or toasted croûtons.

1

2

3

GOES WELL WITH
A spoonful of
crème fraîche
is perfect for
cutting through
the soup with a
slightly acidic
tang.

Chicken Noodle Soup

 SERVES 6   PREP TIME: 5 minutes   COOKING TIME: 30–35 minutes

nutritional information per serving	170 kcals, 2g fat, 0.5g sat fat, 4g total sugars, 0.7g salt

For many, this is the ultimate cure for winter ailments - it's packed with nutritious ingredients and warms you up in no time.

INGREDIENTS

2 skinless chicken breasts

1.2 litres/2 pints chicken stock or water

3 carrots, sliced into 5-mm/¼-inch slices

85 g/3 oz egg noodles

salt and pepper

fresh tarragon leaves, to garnish

1. Place the chicken breasts in a large saucepan over a medium heat, add the stock and bring to a simmer. Cook for 25–30 minutes. Skim any foam from the surface, if necessary. Remove the chicken from the stock and keep warm.

2. Continue to simmer the stock, add the carrots and noodles and cook for 4–5 minutes.

3. Thinly slice or shred the chicken breasts and place in warmed serving bowls.

4. Season the soup to taste with salt and pepper and pour over the chicken. Serve at once, garnished with the tarragon.

COOK'S NOTE
Clean hands are the fastest tools for shredding cooked chicken, flaking cooked fish, crumbling cheese and tearing delicate salad leaves and herbs.

Roast Mediterranean Vegetable Soup

SERVES 6

PREP TIME:
15 minutes
plus standing

COOKING TIME:
2–2¼ hours

nutritional information per serving	173 kcals, 8g fat, 1.5g sat fat, 8g total sugars, 0.7g salt

A real taste of the Mediterranean, with plenty of flavour and little in the way of fat and calories.

INGREDIENTS

2 aubergines
4 tomatoes
2 red peppers
2 onions, unpeeled
2 cloves garlic, unpeeled
4 tbsp olive oil
1 fresh oregano sprig
1.5 litres/2¾ pints chicken or vegetable stock
salt and pepper
chopped fresh basil, to garnish

1. Preheat the oven to 180°C/350°F/Gas Mark 4. Prick the aubergines several times with a fork and put in a roasting tin. Add the tomatoes, peppers and unpeeled onions and garlic. Sprinkle with 2 tablespoons of the oil. Roast in the preheated oven for 30 minutes, then remove the tomatoes. Roast the aubergines, peppers, onions and garlic for a further 30 minutes, until very soft and the pepper skins have blackened.

2. Put the cooked roasted vegetables in a bowl, cover with a damp tea towel and leave for 3–4 hours or overnight, until cold. When cold, cut the aubergines in half, scoop out the flesh and put in the bowl. Remove the skin from the tomatoes, cut in half, discard the seeds and add the flesh to the bowl. Hold the peppers over the bowl to collect the juices and peel off the skin. Remove the stem, core and seeds and add the flesh to the bowl. Peel the onions, cut into quarters and add to the bowl. Squeeze the garlic cloves out of their skin into the bowl.

3. Heat the remaining oil in a large saucepan. Add the vegetables and their juices, the leaves from the oregano sprig, and salt and pepper to taste, then cook gently, stirring frequently, for 30 minutes. Add the stock and bring to the boil, then simmer for 30 minutes.

4. Remove the saucepan from the heat and leave to cool slightly. Transfer to a food processor or blender, in batches if necessary, and process until smooth. Return the soup to the rinsed-out pan and reheat gently; do not boil. Ladle into warmed bowls, garnish with basil and serve immediately.

Carrot, Celery & Apple Soup

 SERVES 4

PREP TIME:
15 minutes

COOKING TIME:
35–40 minutes

nutritional information per serving	174 kcals, 3g fat, 1g sat fat, 31g total sugars, 0.5g salt

A lovely light soup, perfect for days when you want to watch your intake without compromising on taste.

INGREDIENTS

900 g/2 lb carrots, finely diced
1 onion, chopped
3 sticks celery, diced
1 litre/1¾ pints low-salt vegetable stock
2 medium-sized eating apples
2 tbsp tomato purée
1 bay leaf
salt and pepper

to garnish
1 medium-sized eating apple, thinly sliced
juice of ½ lemon
shredded celery leaves

1. Place the carrots, onion and celery in a large saucepan and add the stock. Bring to the boil, reduce the heat, cover and simmer for 10 minutes.

2. Meanwhile, peel, core and dice the apples. Add the diced apple, tomato purée and bay leaf to the saucepan and bring to the boil over a medium heat. Reduce the heat, cover and simmer for 20 minutes. Remove and discard the bay leaf.

3. Meanwhile, to make the garnish, place the apple slices in a small saucepan and pour over the lemon juice. Heat the apple slices gently and simmer for 1–2 minutes, or until the apple is tender. Drain the apple slices and reserve until required.

4. Transfer the carrot and apple mixture to a food processor or blender, in batches if necessary, and process until smooth. Return the soup to the rinsed-out saucepan, reheat gently, and season to taste with salt and pepper. Ladle the soup into warmed bowls, top with the reserved apple slices and shredded celery leaves and serve immediately.

Beef & Barley Broth

 SERVES 8   PREP TIME: 15 minutes   COOKING TIME: 2–2¼ hours

nutritional information per serving	250 kcals, 5.5g fat, 2g sat fat, 5g total sugars, 0.2g salt

Traditionally, in an Irish-style broth, the meat is cut up and divided between individual soup bowls before the broth is poured over. A floury potato for mopping up juices tops each bowl.

INGREDIENTS

650 g/1 lb 7 oz braising beef, in one piece

75 g/2¾ oz pearl barley, rinsed

75 g/2¾ oz green split peas, rinsed

1 large onion, thickly sliced

½ tsp black peppercorns

3 carrots, halved lengthways and sliced

75 g/2¾ oz swede or turnip, diced

1 small leek, green parts included, thinly sliced

1 stick celery, sliced

450 g/1 lb small floury potatoes

75 g/2¾ oz green cabbage, tough core removed and sliced

salt

2 tbsp chopped fresh parsley, to garnish

1. Put the beef, pearl barley and split peas in a large saucepan with the onion and peppercorns. Pour in enough cold water to just cover. Slowly bring to the boil, skim off any foam from the surface, if necessary, then reduce the heat, cover and simmer gently for 1½ hours.

2. Add the carrots, swede, leek and celery to the pan. Season with salt, and simmer for a further 30 minutes. Add a little more water if the soup starts to look too thick.

3. Meanwhile, put the potatoes in another saucepan with water to cover. Add salt to taste and bring to the boil. Cook for 7–10 minutes, until tender but not disintegrating. Drain, return to the pan and cover with a clean kitchen cloth.

4. Remove the meat saucepan from the hob. Carefully lift out the meat using a slotted spoon. Cut into small cubes and return to the pan. Add the cabbage and simmer for a further 5 minutes, or until the cabbage is just tender. Check the seasoning.

5. Ladle the soup into warmed wide soup bowls. Place a potato in the middle of each bowl and sprinkle with the parsley.

Roast Tomato & Pesto Soup

 SERVES 4

PREP TIME:
10 minutes

COOKING TIME:
25–30 minutes

nutritional information per serving	184 kcals, 10.4g fat, 0.6g sat fat, 9g total sugars, 0.6g salt

This soup is a real taste of summer, and a great way to use up a glut of tomatoes from the garden. It's also a light, healthy option, packed with antioxidants, vitamins and minerals.

INGREDIENTS

1 tbsp extra virgin olive oil

2 red onions, cut into small wedges

2 cloves garlic, crushed

700 g/1 lb 9 oz vine ripened tomatoes

500 ml/18 fl oz vegetable stock

salt and pepper

pesto, to garnish

1. Preheat the oven to 200°C/400°F/Gas Mark 6.

2. Place the oil, onions, garlic and tomatoes in a small roasting tin and toss well to coat. Season generously with salt and pepper.

3. Place in the preheated oven for 25–30 minutes, until the tomatoes are starting to blacken and are softened.

4. Process in a blender or food processor together with the stock, until smooth. Taste and adjust the seasoning, if necessary. Reheat gently.

5. Serve each portion of soup drizzled with a little pesto and a pinch of pepper.

2

3

4

Curried Courgette Soup

nutritional information per serving	162 kcals, 9.5g fat, 5.5g sat fat, 6.5g total sugars, 0.4g salt

Make this soup in the height of summer when courgettes are most plentiful and cheap to buy. Adjust the strength of the curry flavour to your own personal taste.

INGREDIENTS

10 g/¼ oz butter
1 large onion, roughly chopped
900 g/2 lb courgettes, sliced
450 ml/16 fl oz vegetable stock
1 tsp curry powder
125 ml/4 fl oz soured cream, plus extra to serve
salt and pepper

1. Melt the butter in a large saucepan over a medium heat. Add the onion and cook for about 3 minutes, until beginning to soften.

2. Add the courgettes, stock and curry powder, then season to taste with salt. Bring the soup to the boil, then reduce the heat, cover and cook gently for about 25 minutes, or until the vegetables are tender.

3. Remove the saucepan from the heat and leave to cool slightly. Transfer to a food processor or blender, in batches if necessary, and process until smooth.

4. Return the soup to the rinsed-out pan, stir in the soured cream and reheat gently; do not boil.

5. Taste and adjust the seasoning, adding salt and pepper if needed. Ladle into warmed bowls, top each with a spoonful of soured cream and serve immediately.

Carrot & Coriander Soup

 SERVES 6

PREP TIME:
15 minutes

COOKING TIME:
35–40 minutes

nutritional information
per serving
205 kcals, 10g fat, 3g sat fat, 9g total sugars, 0.6g salt

This version of the classic soup is made extra special and is packed with flavour by the addition of toasted coriander seeds and lots of fresh coriander.

INGREDIENTS

3 tbsp olive oil
1 red onion, chopped
1 large potato, chopped
1 stick celery, chopped
500 g/1 lb 2 oz carrots, chopped
1 litre/1¾ pints vegetable stock
1 tbsp butter
2 tsp coriander seeds, crushed
1½ tbsp chopped fresh coriander,
plus extra to garnish
225 ml/8 fl oz milk
salt and pepper

1. Heat the oil in a large saucepan. Add the onion and cook over a low heat, stirring occasionally, for 5 minutes, until softened.

2. Add the potato and celery and cook, stirring occasionally, for 5 minutes, then add the carrots and cook for a further 5 minutes. Cover the pan, reduce the heat to very low and cook, shaking the pan occasionally, for 10 minutes.

3. Pour in the stock and bring to the boil, then cover and simmer for 10 minutes, until the vegetables are tender.

4. Meanwhile, melt the butter in a frying pan. Add the coriander seeds and cook, stirring constantly, for 1 minute. Add the chopped coriander and cook, stirring constantly, for 1 minute, then remove from the heat.

5. Remove the soup from the heat and leave to cool slightly. Transfer to a food processor or blender, in batches if necessary, and process until smooth. Return the soup to the rinsed-out pan, stir in the coriander mixture and milk and season to taste with salt and pepper. Reheat gently, then serve, sprinkled with chopped coriander.

Chipotle, Chicken & Bean Soup

SERVES 4

PREP TIME:
5 minutes

COOKING TIME:
20–25 minutes

nutritional information
per serving | 230 kcals, 5.5g fat, 1g sat fat, 12g total sugars, 1.3g salt

A hearty yet simple supper with virtually no preparation, the smoky chipotle heat sits well with the tomatoes and beans to make a rich, thick meal in a bowl.

INGREDIENTS

1 tbsp vegetable oil
1 small onion, finely chopped
2 cloves garlic, crushed
1 tsp whole cumin seeds
1 tbsp chipotle paste, or to taste
1 tbsp tomato purée
85 g/3 oz roasted red peppers, drained and sliced
400 g/14 oz canned chopped tomatoes
200 g/7 oz canned sweetcorn, drained
400 g/14 oz canned cooked kidney beans, drained
150 g/5½ oz cooked chicken, cut into strips
fresh flat-leaf parsley, finely chopped, to serve
salt and pepper

1. Heat the oil in a saucepan over a medium heat and sauté the onion for 3–4 minutes, until starting to soften.

2. Add the garlic and cumin seeds and cook for a further minute, then add the chipotle and tomato purée and cook for 1 minute stirring all the time.

3. Add the peppers and tomatoes and season with salt and pepper. Cover and simmer for 10–15 minutes.

4. Stir in the sweetcorn, kidney beans and chicken and reduce the heat to medium–low. Cook for a further 4–5 minutes. Scatter with parsley to serve.

Spiced Pumpkin Soup

 SERVES 4

PREP TIME:
20 minutes

COOKING TIME:
35–40 minutes

nutritional information
per serving   125 kcals, 6g fat, 1g sat fat, 5.5g total sugars, 0.4g salt

*The perfect use for your Halloween pumpkin - scoop
out the flesh and carve the tough outer left behind.*

INGREDIENTS

2 tbsp olive oil

1 onion, chopped

1 clove garlic, chopped

1 tbsp chopped fresh ginger

1 small red chilli, deseeded and
finely chopped

2 tbsp chopped fresh coriander,
plus extra to garnish

1 bay leaf

900 g/2 lb pumpkin,
deseeded and diced

600 ml/1 pint vegetable stock

salt and pepper

single cream, to garnish

1. Heat the oil in a large saucepan over a medium heat. Add the onion and garlic and cook for about 4 minutes, until slightly softened. Add the ginger, chilli, coriander, bay leaf and pumpkin, and cook for a further 3 minutes.

2. Pour in the stock and bring to a boil. Skim any foam from the surface, if necessary. Reduce the heat and simmer, stirring occasionally, for about 25 minutes, or until the pumpkin is tender. Remove from the heat, discard the bay leaf and leave to cool.

3. Transfer to a food processor or blender, in batches if necessary, and process until smooth. Return the mixture to the rinsed-out pan and season to taste with salt and pepper.

4. Reheat gently, then remove from the heat and pour into warmed soup bowls. Garnish each bowl with a swirl of cream and the coriander, and serve.

1

2

3

COOK'S NOTE
Don't discard the pumpkin seeds, simply rinse and dry, then tip onto a lined baking tray and toss with oil and salt. Cook for 15 minutes at 140°C/275°F/ Gas Mark 1, until golden brown.

Asparagus Soup

 SERVES 6

PREP TIME:
10 minutes

COOKING TIME:
50–55 minutes

nutritional information per serving	240 kcals, 16g fat, 10g sat fat, 5.5g total sugars, 0.6g salt

Best made at the height of the asparagus season, this fresh summer soup is utterly delicious.

INGREDIENTS

1 bunch asparagus, about 350 g/12 oz
700 ml/1¼ pints vegetable stock
55 g/2 oz butter
1 onion, chopped
3 tbsp plain flour
¼ tsp ground coriander
1 tbsp lemon juice
450 ml/16 fl oz milk
4–6 tbsp double or single cream
salt and pepper

1. Wash and trim the asparagus, discarding the woody part of the stem. Cut the remainder into short lengths, reserving the tips for garnish.

2. Cook the asparagus tips in 1 cm/½ inch of boiling water for 5–10 minutes, or until tender. Drain and set aside.

3. Put the asparagus stems in a saucepan with the stock, then bring to the boil, cover and simmer for about 20 minutes, or until the asparagus is soft. Drain the asparagus, reserving the stock.

4. Melt the butter in a saucepan. Add the onion and cook over a low heat for 3–4 minutes, or until soft. Stir in the flour and cook for 1 minute, then gradually whisk in the reserved stock and bring to the boil.

5. Simmer for 2–3 minutes, until thickened, then stir in the cooked asparagus stems, coriander, lemon juice and salt and pepper to taste. Simmer for 10 minutes. Remove the saucepan from the heat and leave to cool slightly. Transfer to a food processor or blender, in batches if necessary, and process until smooth.

6. Return the soup to the rinsed-out pan, add the milk and reserved asparagus tips and bring to the boil. Simmer for 2 minutes. Stir in the cream and reheat gently; do not boil. Ladle into warmed bowls and serve immediately.

Fennel & Summer Vegetable Soup

SERVES 4

PREP TIME:
20 minutes

COOKING TIME:
20–25 minutes

nutritional information per serving	207 kcals, 4g fat, 0.7g sat fat, 4.5g total sugars, 0.8g salt

Beautifully fresh and light, and bursting with the flavours of summer, this soup is a joy to eat, yet sturdy enough to fill you up until dinner.

INGREDIENTS

1 tbsp vegetable oil
1 onion, finely chopped
2 cloves garlic, crushed
1 whole fennel bulb, trimmed and diced
1 leek, finely sliced
1 large potato, diced
1 litre/1¾ pints vegetable stock
100 g/3½ oz spinach, de-stalked
100 g/3½ oz asparagus, trimmed and cut into short lengths
200 g/7 oz frozen peas
handful fresh basil leaves, thinly sliced
salt and pepper

1. Heat the oil in a saucepan over a medium heat and sauté the onion for 5 minutes. Add the garlic, fennel, leek and potato and cook for a further 1–2 minutes.

2. Add the stock and season to taste with salt and pepper. Cover and simmer for 15 minutes.

3. Add the spinach, asparagus and peas and cook for a further 2–3 minutes.

4. Stir in the basil leaves, adjust the seasoning if necessary, and serve.

1

2

3

SOMETHING
DIFFERENT
Try varying
the vegetables
according to the
season. Keep the
base the same
using onion, garlic,
fennel, potato and
leek, but use other
vegetables such
as kale or broad
beans.

Spicy Pepper & Tomato Soup

SERVES 4

PREP TIME: 5 minutes

COOKING TIME: 20–25 minutes

nutritional information per serving	125 kcals, 4g fat, 0.5g sat fat, 13.5g total sugars, 0.5g salt

This vibrant soup is packed with health-boosting antioxidants, plus it's incredibly quick to make as it uses ready-roasted red peppers; a great storecupboard standby for speedy suppers.

INGREDIENTS

1 tbsp vegetable oil

1 onion, chopped

2 cloves garlic, chopped

1½ tsp hot chilli powder

2 tbsp tomato purée

400 g/14 oz roasted red peppers, drained and chopped

2 x 400 g/14 oz canned chopped tomatoes

400 ml/14 fl oz vegetable stock

salt and pepper

1. Heat the oil in a saucepan over a medium heat. Add the onion and garlic and fry for 3–4 minutes, until starting to soften.

2. Add the chilli powder and tomato purée and cook for 1 minute, stirring constantly.

3. Add the red peppers, tomatoes and stock and season to taste with salt and pepper. Stir well, cover and simmer for 15 minutes.

4. Process in a blender or food processor, until smooth. Adjust the seasoning, if necessary, and serve.

2   3   3

GOES WELL WITH
Delicious served
with goat's cheese
crumbled over
the top, and a
generous drizzle
of olive oil.

Lentil & Spinach Soup *68*

Jerusalem Artichoke Soup *70*

Split Pea & Ham Soup *72*

Minestrone Soup *74*

Tomato & White Bean Soup *76*

Italian Meatball Soup *78*

Clam Chowder *80*

Rustic Bread, Basil & Tomato Soup *82*

Potato & Pesto Soup *84*

Spiced Chickpea & Spinach Soup *86*

Chilli Chicken Soup *88*

Cream of Mushroom Soup *90*

Turkey, Sage & Mushroom Soup *92*

Roast Sweet Potato & Garlic Soup *94*

Hearty Soups

Lentil & Spinach Soup

 SERVES 4   PREP TIME: 10 minutes   COOKING TIME: 40–45 minutes

nutritional information per serving	270 kcals, 2.5g fat, 0.5g sat fat, 8g total sugars, 0.9g salt

A beautifully fresh and fragrant soup - light yet packed with flavour and nutrients, simple to make and great to eat at any time of the day.

INGREDIENTS

1 tsp vegetable oil
1 onion, finely chopped
2 cloves garlic, finely chopped
2 sticks celery, finely chopped
200 g/7 oz carrots, finely chopped
½ tsp chilli powder
1 tsp smoked paprika
1 tsp whole cumin seeds
200 g/7 oz red lentils, washed
1 litre/1¾ pints vegetable stock
50 g/1¾ oz spinach, de-stalked and roughly chopped
100 g/3½ oz cherry tomatoes, halved
4 tbsp natural yogurt, to serve
salt and pepper

1. Heat the oil in a large saucepan over a medium heat. Add the onion, garlic, celery and carrots, and cook for 4–5 minutes, or until starting to soften.

2. Add the chilli, paprika and cumin seeds and cook for a further 1 minute, stirring constantly.

3. Add the lentils and stock together with some seasoning, bring to the boil and cook for 10 minutes. Cover and reduce the heat, then simmer for 20–25 minutes until the vegetables and lentils are cooked.

4. Add the spinach and tomatoes and cook for 5 minutes, or until the spinach has wilted. Taste and adjust the seasoning, if necessary. Serve immediately with a tablespoon of yogurt in each bowl.

Jerusalem Artichoke Soup

 SERVES 6

PREP TIME:
10 minutes

COOKING TIME:
45–50 minutes

nutritional information per serving	306 kcals, 21.5g fat, 11.5g sat fat, 4.5g total sugars, 0.8g salt

Jerusalem artichokes lend themselves perfectly to this velvety soup as they break down quickly and easily. Their sweet nutty flavour is delicious with the tangy chives for a wonderfully comforting winter treat.

INGREDIENTS

1 tbsp lemon juice
700 g/1 lb 9 oz Jerusalem artichokes
55 g/2 oz butter
1 tbsp sunflower oil
1 onion, chopped
1.3 litres/2¼ pints vegetable stock
175 ml/6 fl oz milk
1 tbsp snipped fresh chives, plus extra to garnish
100 ml/3½ fl oz double cream
salt and pepper
extra virgin olive oil, for drizzling
croûtons, to serve

1. Fill a bowl with water and stir in the lemon juice. Peel the artichokes and cut into chunks, then immediately drop them into the water to prevent discoloration.

2. Heat the butter with the sunflower oil in a large saucepan. Add the onion and cook over a low heat, stirring occasionally, for 5 minutes, until softened. Drain the artichokes, add them to the pan and stir well. Cover and cook, stirring occasionally, for 15 minutes.

3. Pour in the stock and milk, increase the heat to medium and bring to the boil. Reduce the heat, re-cover the pan and simmer for 20 minutes, until the artichokes are soft.

4. Remove the pan from the heat and leave to cool slightly. Add the chives and transfer the soup to a food processor or blender, in batches if necessary, and process until smooth.

5. Return the soup to the rinsed-out pan, stir in the cream and season to taste with salt and pepper. Reheat gently, then ladle into warmed bowls, drizzle with extra virgin olive oil and serve immediately with the croûtons and chives.

Split Pea & Ham Soup

 SERVES 8

PREP TIME:
10 minutes

COOKING TIME:
1½–1¾ hours

nutritional information per serving	294 kcals, 4.5g fat, 1g sat fat, 3.5g total sugars, 1.2g salt

Although this isn't quick to cook, it is worth waiting for the herbs to release their flavour while cooking.

INGREDIENTS

500 g/1 lb 2 oz split green peas

1 tbsp olive oil

1 large onion, finely chopped

1 large carrot, finely chopped

1 stick celery, finely chopped

1 litre/1¾ pints chicken or vegetable stock

1 litre/1¾ pints water

225 g/8 oz lean smoked ham, finely diced

¼ tsp dried thyme

¼ tsp dried marjoram

1 bay leaf

salt and pepper

1. Rinse the peas under cold running water. Put them in a saucepan and cover with water. Bring to the boil and boil for 3 minutes, skimming any foam from the surface, if necessary. Drain the peas.

2. Heat the oil in a large saucepan over a medium heat. Add the onion and cook for 3–4 minutes, stirring occasionally, until just softened. Add the carrot and celery and continue cooking for 2 minutes.

3. Add the peas, pour over the stock and water and stir to combine.

4. Bring just to the boil and stir the ham into the soup. Add the thyme, marjoram and bay leaf. Reduce the heat, cover and cook gently for 1–1½ hours, until the ingredients are very soft. Remove the bay leaf.

5. Taste and adjust the seasoning. Ladle into warmed soup bowls and serve.

1

2

3

Minestrone Soup

SERVES 4

PREP TIME:
20 minutes

COOKING TIME:
45–50 minutes

nutritional information per serving	352 kcals, 9.5g fat, 2g sat fat, 12.5g total sugars, 1.8g salt

To Italians, minestrone means 'big soup'. It's a great way to use up leftover vegetables and make a wholesome meal big enough to feed a family.

INGREDIENTS

2 tbsp olive oil

2 cloves garlic, chopped

2 red onions, chopped

75 g/2¾ oz Parma ham, sliced

1 red pepper and 1 orange pepper, deseeded and chopped

400 g/14 oz canned chopped tomatoes

1 litre/1¾ pints vegetable stock

1 stick celery, chopped

400 g/14 oz canned borlotti beans, drained and rinsed

100 g/3½ oz green leafy cabbage, shredded

75 g/2¾ oz frozen peas

1 tbsp chopped fresh parsley

75 g/2¾ oz dried vermicelli pasta

salt and pepper

freshly grated Parmesan cheese, to serve

1. Heat the oil in a large saucepan. Add the garlic, onions and ham and cook over a medium heat, stirring, for 3 minutes, until slightly softened.

2. Add the red pepper and orange pepper and the chopped tomatoes and cook for a further 2 minutes, stirring. Stir in the stock, then add the celery.

3. Add the beans to the pan with the cabbage, peas and parsley. Season to taste with salt and pepper. Bring to the boil, then reduce the heat and simmer for 30 minutes.

4. Add the pasta to the pan. Cook for a further 8–10 minutes, or according to the packet instructions. Remove from the heat and ladle into bowls. Sprinkle with Parmesan cheese and serve.

Tomato & White Bean Soup

 SERVES 6

PREP TIME:
30 minutes

COOKING TIME
30–35 minutes

nutritional information per serving	240 kcals, 9g fat, 2.5g sat fat, 12g total sugars, 0.7g salt

This recipe is perfect for using up a glut of tomatoes in the late summer months and is also low in fat.

INGREDIENTS

3 tbsp olive oil

450 g/1 lb red onions, finely chopped

1 stick celery, finely chopped

1 red pepper, deseeded and finely chopped

2 cloves garlic, finely chopped

1 kg/2 lb 4 oz plum tomatoes, peeled and chopped

1.3 litres/2¼ pints vegetable stock

2 tbsp tomato purée

1 tsp sugar

1 tbsp sweet paprika

1 tbsp butter

1 tbsp plain flour

400 g/14 oz canned cooked cannellini beans, drained

salt and pepper

chopped fresh flat-leaf parsley, to garnish

1. Heat the olive oil in a large saucepan. Add the onions, celery, red pepper and garlic and cook over a low heat, stirring occasionally, for 5 minutes, until softened.

2. Increase the heat to medium, add the tomatoes and cook, stirring occasionally, for a further 5 minutes, then pour in the stock. Stir in the tomato purée, sugar and sweet paprika and season to taste with salt and pepper. Bring to the boil, reduce the heat and simmer for 15 minutes.

3. Meanwhile, mash together the butter and flour to a paste in a small bowl with a fork. Stir the paste, small pieces at a time, into the soup. Make sure each piece is fully incorporated before adding the next.

4. Add the beans, stir well and simmer for a further 5 minutes, until heated through. Sprinkle with the parsley and serve immediately.

Italian Meatball Soup

SERVES 6

PREP TIME:
10 minutes

COOKING TIME:
25–30 minutes

nutritional information per serving	260 kcals, 9g fat, 4g sat fat, 1g total sugars, 1.5g salt

A delicious broth with meatballs and mini pasta, this is made into a complete meal with the addition of the greens.

INGREDIENTS

350 g/12 oz lean beef mince

4 tbsp finely grated onion

2 tbsp freshly grated Parmesan cheese, plus extra to serve

1 small egg, beaten

2 litres/3½ pints chicken stock

40 g/1½ oz dried soup pasta

350 g/12 oz Swiss chard or Savoy cabbage, de-stalked and finely shredded

salt and pepper

1. Preheat the oven to 230°C/450°F/Gas Mark 8.

2. Combine the beef, onion, Parmesan, ½ teaspoon of pepper and ¼ teaspoon of salt in a bowl, mixing well with a fork. Stir in the beaten egg. Shape into 24 walnut-sized balls and place on a non-stick baking tray. Cook in the preheated oven for 5–7 minutes, turning once, until lightly coloured. Remove from the oven and set aside.

3. Bring the stock to the boil in a large saucepan. Add the pasta and meatballs, then leave to simmer for 10 minutes.

4. Meanwhile, steam the chard for 2–3 minutes, until wilted. Tip into a sieve and squeeze out as much liquid as possible, pressing with the back of a wooden spoon. Add the chard to the soup and cook for a further 5 minutes, or until the greens and pasta are tender.

5. Taste and adjust the seasoning, adding salt and pepper if needed. Ladle the soup into warmed bowls and serve immediately with Parmesan.

2

3

4

FREEZING TIP
The meatballs can be frozen - simply follow the recipe to the point of making the 24 walnut-sized balls, then place in an airtight container, layer with baking paper, seal and freeze for up to 3 months.

Clam Chowder

SERVES 4   PREP TIME: 15 minutes   COOKING TIME: 25 minutes

nutritional information per serving	890 kcals, 73g fat, 42g sat fat, 6.5g total sugars, 2.7g salt

Delicious classic New-England-style chowder, rich and creamy with a salty hit of bacon, thickened with potatoes.

INGREDIENTS

900 g/2 lb live clams, scrubbed
4 bacon rashers, chopped
2 tbsp butter, plus extra for frying
1 onion, chopped
1 tbsp chopped fresh thyme
1 large potato, diced
300 ml/10 fl oz milk
1 bay leaf
375 ml/13 fl oz double cream
1 tbsp chopped fresh parsley
salt and pepper

1. Place the clams in a large saucepan with a splash of water. Cook over a high heat for 3–4 minutes until they open. Discard any that remain closed. Strain, reserving the cooking liquid. Leave until cool enough to handle, reserving eight for the garnish.

2. Remove the clams from their shells, chopping them roughly if large, and reserve.

3. In a clean saucepan, fry the bacon with a little butter until browned and crisp. Drain on kitchen paper. Add the butter to the same saucepan, and when it has melted, add the onion. Pan-fry for 4–5 minutes until soft but not coloured. Add the thyme and cook briefly before adding the diced potato, reserved clam cooking liquid, milk and bay leaf. Bring to the boil, then reduce the heat and leave to simmer for 10 minutes, or until the potato is just tender.

4. Discard the bay leaf, then transfer to a food processor and process until smooth, or push through a sieve into a bowl.

5. Add the clams, bacon and cream. Simmer for a further 2–3 minutes until heated through. Season to taste with salt and pepper. Stir in the chopped parsley and serve, garnished with the reserved clams in their shells.

Rustic Bread, Basil & Tomato Soup

SERVES 4

PREP TIME: 10 minutes

COOKING TIME: 25–30 minutes

nutritional information per serving : 226 kcals, 6g fat, 2g sat fat, 5.5g total sugars, 1.3g salt

Not only a great way of using up leftover bread, this soup is also a simple supper to whip up if you're in a hurry – with very little prep needed.

INGREDIENTS

1 tbsp olive oil

1 onion, finely chopped

2 cloves garlic, crushed

400 g/14 oz canned whole plum tomatoes

600 ml/1 pint chicken or vegetable stock

200 g/7 oz day-old, unsliced white bread, cubed

handful fresh basil, roughly chopped, plus extra to garnish

salt and pepper

Parmesan cheese, to serve

1. Heat the oil in a saucepan over a medium heat. Add the onion and garlic and sauté for 4–5 minutes.

2. Add the tomatoes and stock, and use the back of a wooden spoon to break the tomatoes apart. Season to taste with salt and pepper, cover and simmer for 15 minutes.

3. Add the bread and basil and simmer for a further 5 minutes.

4. Serve with Parmesan cheese shavings scattered over the top, garnished with the chopped basil and seasoned with pepper to taste.

SOMETHING
DIFFERENT
Use up a glut of
fresh tomatoes -
toss 400 g/
14 oz of them in
a little oil, then
roast in a hot oven
for about
20 minutes.
Add to the soup
in place of the
canned tomatoes.

Potato & Pesto Soup

 SERVES 4   PREP TIME: 20 minutes   COOKING TIME: 40–45 minutes

nutritional information per serving | 1076 kcals, 83g fat, 29g sat fat, 15g total sugars, 1.6g salt

Creamy potatoes and pasta contrast beautifully with home-made pesto to make a fresh-tasting, filling soup.

INGREDIENTS

2 tbsp olive oil

3 rashers rindless smoked bacon, finely chopped

25 g/1 oz butter

450 g/1 lb floury potatoes, chopped

450 g/1 lb onions, finely chopped

600 ml/1 pint chicken stock

600 ml/1 pint milk

100 g/3½ oz dried conchigliette

150 ml/5 fl oz double cream

2 tbsp chopped fresh parsley

salt and pepper

freshly grated Parmesan cheese, to serve

pesto
55 g/2 oz finely chopped fresh parsley

2 cloves garlic, crushed

55 g/2 oz pine nuts, crushed

2 tbsp chopped fresh basil leaves

55 g/2 oz freshly grated Parmesan cheese

150 ml/5 fl oz olive oil

white pepper, to taste

1. To make the pesto, put all of the ingredients in a food processor or blender and process for 2 minutes, to form a rough paste. Scrape into a small bowl and set aside.

2. Heat the oil in a large saucepan and cook the bacon over a medium heat for 4 minutes. Add the butter, potatoes and onions and cook, stirring constantly, for 12 minutes.

3. Add the stock and milk to the saucepan, bring to the boil and simmer for 10 minutes. Add the pasta and simmer for a further 3–4 minutes.

4. Stir in the cream and simmer for 5 minutes. Add the parsley, salt and pepper to taste and 2 tablespoons of the pesto. Ladle the soup into warmed bowls, scatter with Parmesan cheese and serve with the remaining pesto.

Spiced Chickpea & Spinach Soup

SERVES 4   PREP TIME: COOKING TIME:
                5 minutes   20–25 minutes

nutritional information per serving	181 kcals, 6.5g fat, 1g sat fat, 6.5g total sugars, 1g salt

Enjoy a warming blend of aromatic herbs and spices. The addition of the mint dressing makes a delicious, cooling topping that complements the subtle heat of the soup beautifully.

INGREDIENTS

1 tbsp vegetable oil

1 onion, finely chopped

2 cloves garlic, crushed

1 tsp whole cumin seeds

2 tsp medium curry powder

1 tsp hot chilli powder

400 g/14 oz canned cooked chickpeas, drained

400 g/14 oz canned chopped tomatoes

500 ml/18 fl oz vegetable stock

100 g/3½ oz spinach, de-stalked and chopped

salt and pepper

mint dressing

100 g/3½ oz natural yogurt

2 tbsp fresh mint leaves, finely chopped

1. Heat the oil in a saucepan over a medium heat. Add the onion and sauté for 4–5 minutes, or until starting to soften.

2. Add the garlic, cumin seeds, curry and chilli powder and cook for 1 minute, stirring constantly.

3. Add the chickpeas, tomatoes and stock and season to taste with salt and pepper. Bring to the boil, then reduce the heat, cover and simmer for 15 minutes.

4. Meanwhile, to make the mint dressing, mix the yogurt and mint together with salt and pepper, to taste. Cover and chill until ready to serve.

5. Stir the spinach into the soup and cook for a further 1–2 minutes, or until the spinach has wilted. Serve with a little of the mint dressing drizzled over.

Chilli Chicken Soup

 SERVES 4   PREP TIME: 15 minutes   COOKING TIME: 25–30 minutes

nutritional information per serving	251 kcals, 8g fat, 1.5g sat fat, 12g total sugars, 0.8g salt

This deliciously fresh and zingy soup is an explosion of flavours on the palate. It has a light chilli kick which you can adjust to suit your taste.

INGREDIENTS

1 tbsp vegetable oil
1 onion, finely chopped
2 sticks celery, finely chopped
2 carrots, finely chopped
1 red chilli, deseeded and finely chopped
2 cloves garlic, crushed
2 tbsp tomato purée
1 tbsp fresh oregano, finely chopped
600 g/1 lb 5 oz canned whole tomatoes, drained
500 ml/18 fl oz chicken stock
375 g/13 oz chicken breast, cubed
juice of 1 lime
salt and pepper

to garnish
½ bunch spring onions, finely chopped
½ avocado, peeled, stoned and finely chopped
4 tsp chopped fresh coriander
tortilla chips, crumbled

1. Heat the oil in a large saucepan and sauté the onion, celery, carrots, chilli and garlic and cook for 4–5 minutes.

2. Add the tomato purée and cook for a further 1 minute, stirring constantly.

3. Add the oregano, tomatoes and stock and bring to a gentle simmer, breaking down the tomatoes with the back of a wooden spoon to release the juices.

4. Add the chicken and season to taste with salt and pepper, cover and cook for a further 20 minutes.

5. Remove from the heat, stir in the lime juice and ladle the soup into serving bowls. Serve each portion topped with a selection of garnishes.

Cream of Mushroom Soup

 SERVES 4   PREP TIME:
10 minutes
plus cooling
 COOKING TIME:
1½–1¾ hours

nutritional information per serving	600 kcals, 55g fat, 34.5g sat fat, 3g total sugars, 0.7g salt

The secret to this delicious soup is patience. The longer you cook and caramelize the mushrooms in the butter, the deeper and 'meatier' the flavour will be. Take your time and you'll be richly rewarded.

INGREDIENTS

115 g/4 oz unsalted butter

900 g/2 lb white button mushrooms, thickly sliced

1 onion, roughly chopped

1 tbsp flour

1 litre/1¾ pints chicken stock

225 ml/8 fl oz water

6 sprigs fresh thyme, plus picked leaves to garnish

3 cloves garlic

225 ml/8 fl oz double cream

salt and pepper

1. Melt the butter in a large saucepan over a medium heat. Add the mushrooms and a pinch of salt. Cook, stirring occasionally, for 20–30 minutes, or until the mushrooms are golden brown. Reserve some of the browned mushrooms to garnish the soup later.

2. Add the onions and cook over a medium–low heat for about 5 minutes. Add the flour and cook, stirring, for 1 minute. Whisk in the stock and water. Add the thyme and garlic, and bring to a simmer. Reduce the heat to low, cover, and simmer gently for 1 hour.

3. Remove the soup from the heat, uncover, and allow to cool for 15 minutes. Transfer to a food processor or blender, in batches if necessary, and process until smooth.

4. Return the soup to the rinsed-out pan and gently reheat; do not boil. Add the cream, taste and adjust the seasoning, according to taste. Serve hot, topped with the reserved mushrooms and thyme leaves.

Turkey, Sage & Mushroom Soup

 SERVES 6   PREP TIME: 20 minutes   COOKING TIME: 1–1¼ hours

nutritional information per serving	421 kcals, 15g fat, 5.3g sat fat, 2g total sugars, 0.7g salt

Bridging the gap between risotto and stroganoff, this soup is a really filling staple for dinner.

INGREDIENTS

3 tbsp butter

1 onion, finely chopped

1 stick celery, finely chopped

25 large fresh sage leaves, finely chopped

4 tbsp plain flour

1.2 litres/2 pints chicken stock

100 g/3½ oz brown rice

250 g/9 oz mushrooms, sliced

200 g/7 oz cooked turkey, diced

200 ml/7 fl oz double cream

salt and pepper

sprigs of fresh sage, to garnish

freshly grated Parmesan cheese, to serve

1. Melt half the butter in a large saucepan over a medium–low heat. Add the onion, celery and sage and cook for 3–4 minutes, until the onion is softened, stirring frequently. Stir in the flour and continue cooking for 2 minutes.

2. Slowly add about one quarter of the stock and stir well, scraping the bottom of the pan to mix in the flour. Pour in the remaining stock, stirring to combine completely, and bring just to the boil.

3. Stir in the rice and season to taste with salt and pepper. Reduce the heat and simmer gently, partially covered, for about 30 minutes until the rice is just tender, stirring occasionally.

4. Meanwhile, melt the remaining butter in a large frying pan over a medium heat. Add the mushrooms and season to taste with salt and pepper. Cook for about 8 minutes, until they are golden brown, stirring occasionally at first, then more often after they start to colour. Add the mushrooms to the soup.

5. Add the turkey to the soup and stir in the cream. Continue simmering for about 10 minutes, until heated through. Taste and adjust the seasoning, if necessary. Ladle into serving bowls, garnish with sage and serve with Parmesan cheese.

Roast Sweet Potato & Garlic Soup

SERVES 6

PREP TIME:
5 minutes

COOKING TIME:
1¼–1½ hours

nutritional information per serving	226 kcals, 11g fat, 5g sat fat, 9g total sugars, 0.5g salt

This soup has an appetizing combination of colour and taste – roasting the root vegetables intensifies their sweet, earthy flavours.

INGREDIENTS

1 acorn or butternut squash

1 large sweet potato, about 350 g/12 oz

4 shallots

2 tbsp olive oil

6 cloves garlic, unpeeled

850 ml/1½ pints chicken stock

100 ml/3½ fl oz crème fraîche

salt and pepper

snipped fresh chives, to garnish

1. Preheat the oven to 190°C/375°F/Gas Mark 5. Cut the squash, sweet potato and shallots in half lengthwise, through to the stem end. Scoop the seeds out of the squash. Brush a shallow roasting tin with the oil.

2. Place the vegetables, cut-side down, in the prepared tin and add the garlic. Roast in the preheated oven for about 40 minutes until tender and light brown. Set aside and leave to cool.

3. When cool, scoop the flesh from the sweet potato and squash halves and place in a saucepan. Peel the shallots and garlic and add to the other vegetables.

4. Add the stock. Bring just to the boil, reduce the heat and simmer, partially covered, for about 30 minutes, stirring occasionally, until the vegetables are very tender.

5. Leave the soup to cool slightly, then transfer to a food processor and process, in batches if necessary, until smooth.

6. Return the soup to the rinsed-out saucepan. Season with salt and pepper to taste, then simmer for 5–10 minutes, until heated through. Stir in the crème fraîche, then ladle into serving bowls, garnish with snipped chives and serve.

3

6

Around the World

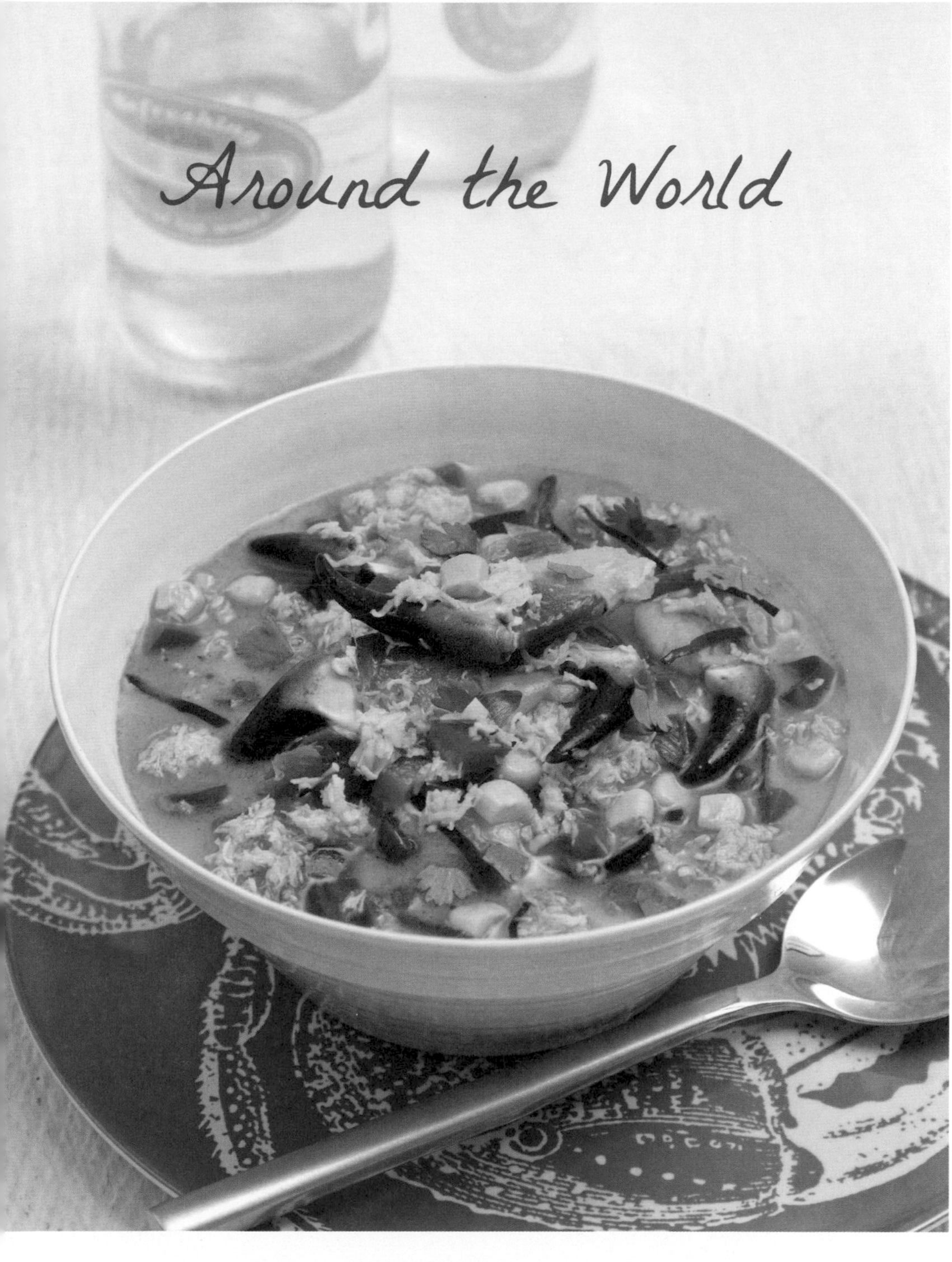

Mexican Vegetable Soup

 SERVES 6

PREP TIME:
25 minutes

COOKING TIME:
35–40 minutes

nutritional information per serving	150 kcals, 5g fat, 0.5g sat fat, 6g total sugars, 0.6g salt

More than just a soup, this is a big bowl bursting with the flavours of Mexico! Inspired by the spices of the country it's a complete meal in a bowl, an explosion of big flavours and colour.

INGREDIENTS

2 tbsp vegetable oil

1 onion, finely chopped

4 cloves garlic, finely chopped

¼–½ tsp ground cumin

2–3 tsp mild chilli powder

1 carrot, sliced

1 waxy potato, diced

350 g/12 oz fresh tomatoes, diced

1 courgette, diced

¼ small head of cabbage, cored and finely shredded

about 1 litre/1¾ pints vegetable or chicken stock, plus extra if necessary

1 fresh corn cob

10 green beans, cut into bite-sized lengths

salt and pepper

chopped fresh coriander and sliced fresh green chilli, to garnish

tortilla chips, to serve

1. Heat the oil in a large saucepan over a medium heat. Add the onion and garlic and cook for 3–4 minutes, until softened, then sprinkle in the cumin and chilli powder. Stir in the carrot, potato, tomatoes, courgette and cabbage and cook, stirring occasionally, for 2 minutes.

2. Pour in the stock. Cover and cook over a medium heat for 20 minutes, or until the vegetables are tender.

3. Meanwhile, remove and discard the husks and silks from the corn cob, then cut off the kernels using a small sharp knife. Add a little extra stock to the soup if needed, then stir in the sweetcorn kernels and beans and cook for a further 5–10 minutes, or until the beans are tender. Season to taste with salt and pepper.

4. Ladle the soup into warmed bowls and garnish with coriander and chilli. Serve immediately with tortilla chips.

Wonton Soup

 SERVES 6

PREP TIME:
10 minutes
plus marinading

COOKING TIME:
5–10 minutes

nutritional information per serving	122 kcals, 3g fat, 1g sat fat, 2g total sugars, 1.4g salt

The little Chinese parcels are lightly poached in the soup broth to give a tender finish.

INGREDIENTS

175 g/6 oz minced pork or chicken

55 g/2 oz peeled prawns, minced

1 spring onion, finely chopped

1 tsp finely chopped fresh ginger

1 tsp sugar

1 tbsp Chinese rice wine or dry sherry

2 tbsp light soy sauce

24 ready-made wonton wrappers

850 ml/1½ pints vegetable stock

snipped fresh chives, to garnish

1. Mix together the pork, prawns, spring onion, ginger, sugar, rice wine and half the soy sauce in a bowl until thoroughly combined. Cover and leave to marinate for 20 minutes.

2. Put 1 teaspoon of the mixture in the centre of each wonton wrapper. Dampen the edges, fold corner to corner into a triangle and press to seal, then seal the two remaining corners together.

3. Bring the stock to the boil in a large saucepan. Add the wontons and cook for 5 minutes. Stir in the remaining soy sauce and remove from the heat. Ladle the soup and wontons into warmed bowls, sprinkle with snipped chives and serve immediately.

1

2

3

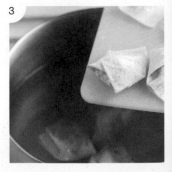

FREEZING TIP
Make the wonton parcels in advance by following steps 1 and 2. Then place on a lined baking tray and put in the freezer. Once frozen, transfer to an airtight container and store for up to 3 months.

Lobster Bisque

 SERVES 4   PREP TIME: 30 minutes   COOKING TIME: 45–50 minutes

nutritional information per serving	454 kcals, 24g fat, 14g sat fat, 5g total sugars, 1.1g salt

This elegant, smooth and delicious soup is perfect for entertaining and bound to impress your guests.

INGREDIENTS

450 g/1 lb cooked lobster
40 g/1½ oz butter
1 small carrot, grated
1 stick celery, finely chopped
1 leek, finely chopped
1 small onion, finely chopped
2 shallots, finely chopped
3 tbsp brandy or Cognac
50 ml/2 fl oz dry white wine
1.2 litres/2 pints water
1 tbsp tomato purée
125 ml/4 fl oz whipping cream, or to taste
6 tbsp plain flour
2–3 tbsp cold water
salt and pepper
snipped fresh chives, to garnish

1. Pull off the lobster tail. With the legs up, cut the body in half lengthways. Scoop out the tomalley and the roe. Reserve these, cover and chill in the refrigerator. Remove the meat from the rest of the lobster and cut into bite-sized pieces, then cover and chill in the refrigerator. Chop the shell into large pieces.

2. Melt half the butter in a large saucepan over a medium heat and add the lobster shell pieces. Fry until brown bits begin to stick on the bottom of the pan. Add the carrot, celery, leek, onion and shallots. Cook, stirring constantly, for 1–2 minutes. Add the brandy and wine and simmer for 1 minute. Pour over the water, add the tomato purée and a large pinch of salt, and bring to the boil. Reduce the heat and simmer for 30 minutes, then strain the stock, discarding the solids.

3. Melt the remaining butter in a small saucepan and add the tomalley and roe. Add the cream and whisk to mix well, then remove from the heat and set aside. Put the flour in a small mixing bowl and very slowly whisk in the cold water. Stir in a little of the hot stock mixture to make a smooth liquid.

4. Bring the remaining lobster stock to the boil and whisk in the flour mixture. Boil gently for 4–5 minutes, or until the soup thickens. Press the tomalley, roe and cream mixture through a sieve into the soup, then add the lobster meat. Simmer until heated through.

5. Taste and adjust the seasoning, adding salt and pepper if needed. Stir in a little more cream if wished. Ladle into warmed bowls, garnish with chives and serve immediately.

Avocado Soup
with Guacamole Croûtes

SERVES 6   PREP TIME: 15 minutes   COOKING TIME: 30–35 minutes

nutritional information per serving	476 kcals, 39g fat, 15g sat fat, 3.5g total sugars, 1g salt

Cooking the avocado brings out its buttery sweetness, which contrasts with crispy-textured croûtes.

INGREDIENTS

3 ripe avocados
2 tbsp lemon juice
85 g/3 oz butter
6 shallots, chopped
1½ tbsp plain flour
850 ml/1½ pints vegetable stock
175 ml/6 fl oz single cream
salt and pepper
extra virgin olive oil, for drizzling
1 lime, thinly sliced, to garnish

guacamole croûtes
6 thin slices of day-old baguette
olive oil, for brushing
½ large ripe avocado, stoned and brushed with lime juice
juice of 1 lime
½ tsp hot pepper sauce, or to taste

1. Halve the avocados lengthways and gently twist the halves apart. Remove and discard the stones and scoop out the flesh. Chop into small pieces, put them into a bowl, sprinkle with the lemon juice and toss well to coat.

2. Melt the butter in a saucepan. Add the shallots and cook over a low heat, stirring occasionally, for 5 minutes, until softened. Stir in the flour and cook, stirring constantly, for 1 minute. Remove the pan from the heat and gradually stir in the stock. Return the pan to medium heat and bring to the boil, stirring constantly.

3. Add the chopped avocado, reduce the heat, cover and simmer for 15 minutes.

4. Meanwhile, to make the guacamole croûtes, preheat the grill. Toast the bread on one side under the preheated grill. Turn the slices over, brush with oil and toast the second side. Remove from the heat. Scoop out the avocado flesh into a bowl and mash with the lime juice and hot pepper sauce and season to taste with salt and pepper. Divide the avocado mixture between the croûtes and set aside.

5. Remove the soup from the heat and push it through a strainer set over a bowl. Return the strained soup to the rinsed-out pan, stir in the cream, and reheat gently; do not boil. Season to taste with salt and pepper.

6. Ladle the soup into warmed bowls, drizzle with olive oil and garnish with the lime slices. Serve with the guacamole croûtes.

Chicken & Mushroom Soup with Puff Pastry

SERVES 4

PREP TIME:
10 minutes

COOKING TIME:
1–1¼ hours

nutritional information
per serving

716 kcals, 37g fat, 18.5g sat fat, 4g total sugars, 1.8g salt

The base of this soup is an infusion of cider and chicken stock that's delicious with the pastry top.

INGREDIENTS

2 chicken legs, skin removed
1 litre/1¾ pints chicken stock
150 ml/5 fl oz dry cider
1 onion, finely chopped
1 bay leaf
250 g/9 oz chestnut mushrooms, thickly sliced
4 tbsp cornflour blended with 4 tbsp water
4 tbsp crème fraîche
salt and pepper
flour, for sprinkling
500 g/1 lb 2 oz ready-made puff pastry

1. Place the chicken legs in a large saucepan with the stock, cider, onion and bay leaf. Place over a medium heat, cover and simmer for 25 minutes. Add the mushrooms and simmer for a further 10 minutes. Remove the chicken and set aside. Remove and discard the bay leaf.

2. Stir the cornflour into the stock. Heat, stirring constantly, until boiling and thickened. Remove from the heat and leave to cool. Remove the meat from the chicken legs and tear into pieces.

3. Preheat the oven to 200°C/400°F/Gas Mark 6. Stir the chicken and crème fraîche into the soup. Season to taste with salt and pepper then ladle into ovenproof bowls. They should be about three quarters full.

4. Lightly flour a work surface then roll out the pastry. Cut out rounds or squares large enough to cover the tops of the bowls with a 1 cm/½ inch overlap. Brush the rim of each bowl with water, lay the pastry on top, press around the rim and pierce the centres. Bake in the preheated oven for 20–25 minutes, or until the pastry is golden. Serve immediately.

1
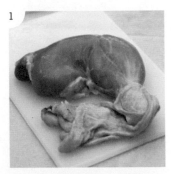

1

4

HEALTHY HINT
Of course, you
could always
remove the
pastry to
save on calories
and swap to a
reduced fat crème
fraîche for a
lighter alternative.

Clam & Pasta Soup

 SERVES 6

PREP TIME:
10 minutes

COOKING TIME:
30–35 minutes

nutritional information per serving | 212 kcals, 6.5g fat, 1g sat fat, 6.5g total sugars, 0.8g salt

A great way to feed a hungry crowd using fresh clams, which are usually fairly inexpensive. Make sure you have some warm crusty bread at the ready to mop up all the delicious flavours.

INGREDIENTS

3 tbsp olive oil

1 Spanish onion, finely chopped

3 cloves garlic, finely chopped

600 g/1 lb 5 oz canned chopped tomatoes

2 tbsp tomato purée

2 tsp sugar

1 tsp dried oregano

1 litre/1¾ pints vegetable stock

500 g/1 lb 2 oz live clams, scrubbed

175 ml/6 fl oz dry white wine

85 g/3 oz dried conchigliette

3 tbsp chopped fresh flat-leaf parsley

salt and pepper

1. Heat the oil in a large saucepan. Add the onion and garlic and cook over a low heat, stirring occasionally, for 5 minutes, until softened. Add the tomatoes, tomato purée, sugar, oregano and stock and season with salt and pepper. Mix well and bring to the boil, then reduce the heat, cover and simmer, stirring occasionally, for 5 minutes.

2. Discard any clams with broken shells and any that refuse to close when tapped. Put the clams into a saucepan, pour in the wine, cover and cook over a high heat, shaking the pan occasionally, for 3–5 minutes.

3. Remove the pan from the heat and, using a slotted spoon, transfer the clams to a bowl. Reserve the cooking liquid. Discard any clams that remain closed and remove the remainder from the half shells. Strain the reserved cooking liquid through a sieve into a bowl and set aside.

4. Add the pasta to the soup and simmer, uncovered, for 10 minutes. Add the cooked clams and the reserved cooking liquid. Stir well and heat gently for 4–5 minutes; do not allow the soup to come back to the boil. Taste and adjust the seasoning, if necessary, stir in the parsley and serve immediately.

Roast Pumpkin, Garlic & Thyme Soup

 SERVES 6

PREP TIME:
10 minutes

COOKING TIME:
1¼–1½ hours

nutritional information per serving	310 kcals, 20g fat, 8g sat fat, 8.5g total sugars, 0.6g salt

Oven roasting the garlic bulbs brings out the sweetness and adds flavour to this classic soup with a twist.

INGREDIENTS

4 tbsp olive oil, plus extra for drizzling

2 bulbs garlic

900 g/2 lb pumpkin or butternut squash

2 tbsp fresh thyme leaves, plus extra sprigs to garnish

25 g/1 oz butter

1 onion, chopped

1 tbsp plain flour

1.2 litres/2 pints chicken stock

100 g/3½ oz crème fraîche

salt and pepper

1. Preheat the oven to 190°C/375°F/Gas Mark 5. Pour ½ tablespoon of the oil over each garlic bulb and sprinkle with salt and pepper to taste, then wrap in aluminium foil and place in a large roasting tin. Peel and deseed the pumpkin, then cut the flesh into large chunks. Toss the pumpkin in the remaining oil and sprinkle with salt and pepper to taste and half the thyme leaves. Place in the roasting tin in a single layer and cook in the preheated oven for 1 hour.

2. Melt the butter in a large saucepan. Add the onion and cook over a medium heat, stirring occasionally, for 5 minutes, until soft. Stir in the flour and cook for 2 minutes. Add the stock, a few spoonfuls at a time to begin with, then add the remainder, stirring constantly.

3. When the pumpkin has browned, remove the roasting tin from the oven. Add the pumpkin to the pan and simmer for 10 minutes.

4. Open the garlic packages and leave to cool. When cool enough to handle, break up the garlic bulbs, place the cloves on a chopping board and press down on each until the garlic pulp squeezes out.

5. Remove the soup from the heat and leave to cool slightly. Stir in the garlic pulp and the remaining thyme leaves, then transfer to a food processor or blender, in batches if necessary, and process until smooth. Return the soup to the rinsed-out pan and reheat gently; do not boil.

6. Ladle into warmed bowls and top each with a spoonful of the crème fraîche. Drizzle over a little oil, garnish with thyme sprigs and serve immediately.

Borscht

nutritional information per serving   252 kcals, 10g fat, 6g sat fat, 22g total sugars, 1.1g salt

Originally from Ukraine, this sweet and sour soup based on beetroot and tomatoes and flavoured with fresh bouquet garni is popular in many Eastern and central European countries too.

INGREDIENTS

5 raw beetroots, about 1 kg/2 lb 4 oz

70 g/2½ oz butter

2 onions, thinly sliced

3 carrots, thinly sliced

3 sticks celery, thinly sliced

6 tomatoes, peeled, deseeded and chopped

1 tbsp red wine vinegar

1 tbsp sugar

2 cloves garlic, finely chopped

1 bouquet garni (3 fresh parsley sprigs, 2 fresh thyme sprigs and 1 bay leaf, tied together)

1.3 litres/2¼ pints vegetable stock

salt and pepper

soured cream and chopped fresh dill, to garnish

1. Peel and coarsely grate four of the beetroots. Melt the butter in a large saucepan. Add the onions and cook over a low heat, stirring occasionally, for 5 minutes, until softened. Add the grated beetroots, carrots and celery and cook, stirring occasionally, for a further 5 minutes.

2. Increase the heat to medium, add the tomatoes, vinegar, sugar, garlic and bouquet garni, season with salt and pepper and stir well, then pour in the stock and bring to the boil. Reduce the heat, cover and simmer for 1¼ hours.

3. Meanwhile, peel and grate the remaining beetroot. Add it and any juices to the pan and simmer for a further 10 minutes. Remove the pan from the heat and leave to stand for 10 minutes.

4. Remove and discard the bouquet garni. Ladle the soup into warmed bowls and top each with a spoonful of soured cream, sprinkle with chopped dill and serve immediately.

Miso Soup

SERVES 2   PREP TIME: 10 minutes   COOKING TIME: 15–20 minutes

nutritional information per serving	154 kcals, 7g fat, 0.8g sat fat, 1g total sugars, 2.7g salt

Miso is a highly nutritious staple in Japan, made from fermented soya beans. Together with barley or rice, it adds a unique umami-based flavour.

INGREDIENTS

1 litre/1¾ pints water

2 tsp dashi granules

175 g/6 oz silken tofu, drained and cut into small cubes

4 shiitake mushrooms, finely sliced

4 tbsp miso paste

2 spring onions, chopped

1. Put the water in a large pan with the dashi granules and bring to the boil. Add the tofu and mushrooms, reduce the heat, and let simmer for 3 minutes.

2. Stir in the miso paste and let simmer gently, stirring, until the miso has dissolved.

3. Add the spring onions and serve immediately. If you leave the soup, the miso will settle, so give the soup a thorough stir before serving to recombine.

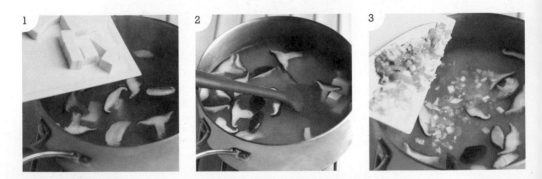

1   2   3

SOMETHING
DIFFERENT
If you don't
have shiitake
mushrooms then
use large field
mushrooms which
are more readily
available.

Crab & Ginger Soup

 SERVES 4

PREP TIME:
10 minutes

COOKING TIME:
25–30 minutes

nutritional information per serving	363 kcals, 16g fat, 5g sat fat, 6g total sugars, 1.7g salt

The rich crabmeat is offset perfectly by the aromatic ginger, sweet coconut milk and fresh lime juice and rind to make a tasty Thai-inspired soup.

INGREDIENTS

2 tbsp chilli oil

1 clove garlic, chopped

4 spring onions, trimmed and sliced

2 red peppers, deseeded and chopped

1 tbsp grated fresh ginger

1 litre/1¾ pints fish stock

100 ml/3½ fl oz coconut milk

100 ml/3½ fl oz rice wine or sherry

2 tbsp lime juice

1 tbsp grated lime rind

6 young kaffir lime leaves, finely shredded

300 g/10½ oz freshly cooked crabmeat

200 g/7 oz freshly cooked crab claws

150 g/5½ oz canned sweetcorn, drained

1 tbsp of chopped fresh coriander, plus a few sprigs to garnish

salt and pepper

1. Heat the oil in a large saucepan over a medium heat. Add the garlic and spring onions and cook, stirring, for about 3 minutes, until slightly softened. Add the red peppers and ginger and cook for a further 4 minutes, stirring.

2. Pour in the stock and season to taste with salt and pepper. Bring to the boil, then reduce the heat. Pour in the coconut milk, rice wine and lime juice, and stir in the grated lime rind and kaffir lime leaves. Simmer for 15 minutes.

3. Add the crabmeat and crab claws to the soup with the sweetcorn and coriander. Cook the soup for 5 minutes, or until the crab is heated through.

4. Remove from the heat. Ladle into warmed soup bowls, garnish with sprigs of coriander and serve immediately.

Salmon Ramen Soup

 SERVES 4

PREP TIME:
10 minutes

COOKING TIME:
20–25 minutes

nutritional information per serving	500 kcals, 19g fat, 3.5g sat fat, 5g total sugars, 2.9g salt

In this recipe, the salmon is grilled in a sweet sticky teriyaki marinade and served on a bowl of oriental spiced broth with egg noodles. It's warming, satisfying and easy to prepare.

INGREDIENTS

1 litre/1¾ pints vegetable stock
1 clove garlic
½ tsp light soy sauce
4 salmon fillets, about 140 g/5 oz each, skinned
sunflower oil, for brushing
140 g/5 oz dried ramen noodles
100 g/3½ oz baby spinach leaves
4 spring onions, finely chopped

teriyaki glaze
2½ tbsp sake
2½ tbsp dark soy sauce
2 tbsp mirin or sweet sherry
½ tbsp soft light brown sugar
½ clove garlic, very finely chopped
5-mm/¼-inch piece fresh ginger, very finely chopped

to serve
100 g/3½ oz fresh beansprouts
1 fresh green chilli, deseeded and sliced
fresh coriander leaves

1. Preheat the grill to high. Put the stock in a saucepan, add the garlic clove and soy sauce and bring to the boil.

2. Mix together the ingredients for the teriyaki glaze and brush one surface of each salmon fillet with the glaze. Lightly brush the grill rack with oil and cook the salmon under the preheated grill for 4 minutes on one side only. The fish should be almost cooked through and flake easily. Remove from the grill and set aside.

3. Meanwhile, cook the noodles in a saucepan of boiling water for 5 minutes, or according to the packet instructions, until tender. Drain the noodles, then cover and set aside.

4. Remove the garlic from the stock, then bring the stock back to the boil. Drop in the spinach leaves and spring onions and cook until the leaves are just wilted. Use a slotted spoon to remove the spinach and spring onions from the pan and divide them between warmed bowls. Divide the noodles between the bowls, then add a salmon fillet to each. Carefully pour the boiling stock into each bowl.

5. Sprinkle with the beansprouts, chilli and coriander leaves and serve immediately.

French Onion Soup

 SERVES 6   PREP TIME: 30 minutes   COOKING TIME: 1½ hours

nutritional information per serving	480 kcals, 23g fat, 11g sat fat, 7.5g total sugars, 2.2g salt

Traditionally a soup served throughout the night to workers at the famous Les Halles market in Paris.

INGREDIENTS

675 g/1 lb 8 oz onions

3 tbsp olive oil

4 cloves garlic, 3 chopped and 1 kept whole

1 tsp sugar

2 tsp chopped fresh thyme, plus extra sprigs to garnish

2 tbsp plain flour

125 ml/4 fl oz dry white wine

2 litres/3½ pints vegetable stock

6 slices French bread

300 g/10½ oz Gruyère cheese, grated

1. Thinly slice the onions. Heat the oil in a large, heavy-based saucepan over a medium–low heat, add the onions and cook, stirring occasionally, for 10 minutes, or until they are just beginning to brown. Stir in the chopped garlic, sugar and chopped thyme, then reduce the heat and cook, stirring occasionally, for 30 minutes, or until the onions are golden brown.

2. Sprinkle in the flour and cook, stirring constantly, for 1–2 minutes. Stir in the wine. Gradually stir in the stock and bring to the boil, skimming off any foam that rises to the surface, then reduce the heat and simmer for 45 minutes. Meanwhile, preheat the grill to medium–high. Toast the bread on both sides under the grill, then rub the toast with the whole garlic clove.

3. Ladle the soup into six flameproof bowls set on a baking tray. Float a piece of toast in each bowl and divide the grated cheese between them. Place under the grill for 2–3 minutes, or until the cheese has just melted. Garnish with thyme sprigs and serve at once.

1

2

3

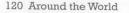

SOMETHING
DIFFERENT
Try using red
onions for a
slightly sweeter,
milder flavour.

Vietnamese Crab Soup

 SERVES 6

PREP TIME:
10 minutes
plus soaking

COOKING TIME:
15–20 minutes

nutritional information per serving	288 kcals, 11g fat, 1.5g sat fat, 1.5g total sugars, 2.6g salt

Light, clean and fresh, this broth is quick and simple to make and perfect to kick off an Asian-style meal.

INGREDIENTS

6 dried shiitake mushrooms

350 ml/12 fl oz hot water

5 spring onions

350 g/12 oz asparagus spears, trimmed

750 g/1 lb 10 oz white crabmeat, thawed if frozen

2 tbsp groundnut oil

3 cloves garlic, finely chopped

1.7 litres/3 pints vegetable stock

1–2 tbsp Thai fish sauce

3 tbsp chopped fresh coriander

1. Put the mushrooms into a bowl, pour in the water and leave to soak for 20 minutes. Meanwhile, chop the white parts of the spring onions and thinly slice the green parts diagonally. Slice the asparagus diagonally into 2-cm/¾-inch pieces. Pick over the crabmeat and remove any pieces of shell and cartilage.

2. Drain the mushrooms, reserving the soaking liquid, and squeeze gently to remove the excess liquid. Remove and discard the stalks and thinly slice the caps. Strain the soaking liquid through a muslin-lined strainer.

3. Heat the oil in a large saucepan. Add the chopped spring onions and garlic and stir-fry over a medium heat for 2 minutes. Pour in the stock and reserved soaking liquid, add the mushrooms and bring to the boil.

4. Stir in 1 tablespoon of the Thai fish sauce, add the sliced spring onions and asparagus pieces and bring back to the boil. Reduce the heat and simmer for 5 minutes, then gently stir in the crabmeat and coriander. Simmer for a further 3–4 minutes to heat through.

5. Remove the pan from the heat, taste and stir in more fish sauce, if necessary. Ladle into warmed bowls and serve immediately.

Mixed Bean Soup with Gruyère

 SERVES 4 | PREP TIME: 15 minutes | COOKING TIME: 50–55 minutes

nutritional information per serving | 473 kcals, 29g fat, 16g sat fat, 9g total sugars, 1.8g salt

Full of beans, vegetables and fresh herbs, and finished with tangy cheese, this will leave you wanting more!

INGREDIENTS

1 tbsp olive oil

3 cloves garlic, finely chopped

4 spring onions, sliced, plus extra to garnish

200 g/7 oz mushrooms, sliced

1 litre/1¾ pints vegetable stock

1 large carrot, chopped

400 g/14 oz canned mixed beans, drained and rinsed

800 g/1 lb 12 oz canned chopped tomatoes

1 tbsp chopped fresh thyme

1 tbsp chopped fresh oregano

175 g/6 oz Gruyère cheese, grated

4 tbsp double cream, plus extra to serve

salt and pepper

1. Heat the oil in a large saucepan over a medium heat. Add the garlic and spring onions and cook, stirring, for 3 minutes, until slightly softened. Add the mushrooms and cook, stirring, for a further 2 minutes.

2. Stir in the stock, then add the carrot, beans, tomatoes and herbs. Season to taste with salt and pepper. Bring to the boil, then reduce the heat and simmer for 30 minutes.

3. Remove the soup from the heat and leave to cool slightly. Transfer to a food processor or blender, in batches if necessary, and process until smooth.

4. Return the soup to the rinsed-out pan and stir in the cheese. Cook for a further 10 minutes, then stir in the cream. Cook for 5 minutes, then remove from the heat. Ladle into warmed bowls, top each with a swirl of cream and garnish with spring onions. Serve immediately.

1

2

4

HEALTHY HINT
If you are watching calories and fat content, then swap the double cream for low-fat crème fraîche and use just a scattering of Gruyère.

Index